NIGHT CRIES

Also by John Cassidy

The Dancing Man (Poet's Yearbook, 1977)
An Attitude of Mind (Hutchinson, 1978)
Changes of Light (Bloodaxe, 1979)
The Fountain (Bloodaxe, 1979)

NIGHT CRIES

John Cassidy

BLOODAXE BOOKS

ISBN: 0 906427 45 2

First published 1982 by
Bloodaxe Books Ltd,
P.O. Box 1SN,
Newcastle upon Tyne NE99 1SN.

The publisher acknowledges the financial assistance
of Northern Arts.

Typesetting & cover printing by
Tyneside Free Press Workshop Ltd, Newcastle upon Tyne.

Printed in Great Britain by
Unwin Brothers Ltd, Old Woking, Surrey.

For Catherine, Stephen and Noel

Acknowledgements

Some of these poems were published in two Bloodaxe pamphlets, *Changes of Light* and *The Fountain* (1979). *The Fountain* was a re-issue of those poems from John Cassidy's booklet *The Dancing Man* (Poet's Yearbook Award, 1977) which were not included in his book *An Attitude of Mind* (Hutchinson, 1978).

Acknowledgements are due to the editors of the following publications in which some of the poems have appeared: *Critical Quarterly, Dragoncards 12* (Mandeville Press), *The Honest Ulsterman*, *Megaphone*, *New Poetry 2* and *3* (Arts Council, 1976 and 1977), *New Poetry 4* (Hutchinson/Arts Council—P.E.N., 1978), *Other Poetry*, *Outposts*, *Palantir*, *Poetry Review*, *Poetry Survey*, *Stand*, and *Workshop New Poetry*. 'Poulter's Hare', 'The Royal Charter', 'Scotchman's Stump' and 'Tom Robinson' were broadcast on *Poetry Now* (BBC Radio 3); other poems were read on the N.W. Arts/British Telecom 'Dial-a-Poem' scheme.

Contents

January Trees

At the low point of the year
with trees little more than logs
up-ended and embedded
in a soil like concrete, moss

of a strident green smothers
each bole in horizontal
afternoon sunlight. There are
days when snow plasters one half

white, upwind, and the other
glows in its pelisse of moss.
And I consider whether
trees are notable only

for what they carry, even
in winter, or whether they
stand, themselves in themselves, stark,
being sufficiently trees.

It could be that display is
here a function of living,
bodying out the virtue
of holding the white and green

apart and together, as,
in two months, splutters of leaves
will admit complicity,
will hide and hatch out birdsong.

Night Cries

Peacocks yelp in the dark through
Half a mile of wood. The night
Twitches with petulance. They stalk
Over the soft moss of their enclosure,
Jabbing at the protective
Wire.
      On the other side of the house
Across open marshland, a pair
Of redshank lift on their free wings and wail
In widening rings of bewilderment
Round where a lank marauding stoat,
Loose from the peacocks' cloistered wood,
Sniffs, splits and sucks up their four blotched eggs.

Contacts

It is not my first failure.
There is no need to look away or stand
Shifting the silence from foot to foot.
I am stubborn about these things.

I had a claw-grip on the trunk
I thought unshakable as an owl's.
I looked to the friction of a rough
Foot to stick me to the bark for ever.

As always I discounted
The change of season. Owl images,
A darkness hung with wide eyes,
A quavering claim on the night,

Hold no sway in the noon city
Summering the tar to a tacky
Shoe-trap. The itch and sweat of streets
Tangled with purposeful struggle

Ought to enmesh my attention. Yet
There is something missing from these bright
Energies, as if what matters
Is in abeyance, waiting for dark.

To stroll through cooling suburbs
Leisurely into a dusk wood
Must be an abdication, acceptance
Of loss. It feels like a search.

Ancient dwellers among trees are long
Contracted into curiosities,
Dealers in fringe legends. I enter,
Homing in on the house of the last witch.

Poulter's Hare

His looking startled is a trick
Of the domed eyes sticking outwards
So that he can see behind him,
Running.

He looks that way even when dead.
When just dead. Later, hung
Up by the heels and bleeding
Pell-mell into a tin cup on his nose,
He seems more used to his changed
Condition, hardly surprised
At all.

He has such a chequered
Reputation. In some tales
The familiar of frightful women,
With dimensions of darkness and fire,
A thing to stay clear of.
Or the crazy, moon-linked unpredictable
Leaper, living in myth and on ploughland,
Daubed on palaeolithic cave-walls,
Flickering through dreams.

In daylight, the distant trembler, ears like
Aerials above the corn,
A bolt to be triggered
By the tread of a fly.
He can slip two counties behind him
Given a clear start.

With those out-of-proportion long
Hind legs he runs uphill straight
To outpace any slavering dog,
Doubles back along wall-tops, baffling
Beagles' noses, whitens in winter
In northern hills, full
Of ruses.

For centuries a legend-maker,
He has lived inside heads, exactly
The place for a fast, fearful
Eruption from nowhere, a bewildering
Twist in the arrow's logic, hazed
In secrets, intricate dancer
Over the uncompromising earth,
Vanishing as if never there.

A blood-pumped, bounding imponderable,
Packed in this minutely mottled fur.

Disturbance

I woke when a magpie hammered
Its machine-gun voice from close range
Into my ear as if in the same room.
A sharp light marked the first break
Of the first morning in June, the sky
A whole smooth eggshell.

The magpie was smashing a sparrow's nest
Above the window, pick-axing through
To the bald, reptilian young.
Three days hatched, they were spiked
Out of that lined, close world by a black
Bill and an implacable eye.

All their last energy went in a frenzy
Of wheezing. One was lifted fifty yards
Away to a bough and banged and broken
And gulped. It was there to be seen but I saw
In my mind and lay close under blankets
Unmoving, thinking of instability

And how it seems to live in another
Medium, unseen, unknown, outside,
Till the great beak crashes in.
Knowing it is no benefit. I hear
The black-white-black flap of that magpie
Come chattering back for the next grab.

Powers

A thousand glinting feet below me
On the lake a waterskier
Stiffly swings across and back
Across and back over the wake
Widening from his speedboat.

Below me too, a hundred feet or so,
A buzzard floats into the morning,
Swinging a slow arc across and back
Across and back over the mountain
The metal water and the zipping boats.

The mottled wings blot out a moment
Skier and spray. The fanned feathers,
Soft, moth-coloured, smother
The jagged glare, almost nullify
The snarl, the imagined taint of oil.

His domination is of a second
Only. From that coincidence
Of curves the riders drag apart.
The waterskier wheels away
Grandly visible to a ring of summits.

Above, the inconspicuous bird
Balances, then glides briefly to the grass:
This too an imposing of aggressive skill,
Attested by the squeaking of a vole
That dangles now from one disdainful claw.

Intersection

Morning traffic heading north
panted and grumbled past
over the bridge, thickening quickly,
blocking entries; houses were letting
people out, and dogs sniffed
through gates and stretched into a new day.

The labouring wag of grey
wings, wide and curving,
delivered a solitary heron
over traffic and chimneys,
bill jutting like a fighter's radar,
legs neatly together out behind the tail.

The wingbeat's steady flail
at two to a second carried
the tucked neck like a passenger
without tension or hesitations,
crossing the traffic flow to where
miles away standing water waited.

His buoyant passing-by restated
the antique conflict. Over all
the moaning pantechnicons
clinging to their curving routes
his free eye glittered, catching
a distant shine beyond the reeds.

That lone flight left seeds
of seductive images: the old
survivor, hauling himself about
his different business, invading
even the centre, an unplanned presence.
The growing day ground them between its teeth.

An Inconvenience

Quite early in the night, close,
Moonless and in a place where no
Lamp-posts made things normal,
Where no traffic swung its flow
Of lights, there came a small
Uneasy scraping near the house.

Under the window grass grew tall,
And blackberries. Amongst them, living,
A long unrhythmic movement brushed at
The silence and disturbed nothing.
Torchlight, pointed down, neither hushed it
Nor discovered a hair of anything at all.

It seemed a muscled creature, shifting its mystery.
Whatever its name it was a forbidden
Thing, fox, badger, even otter,
Supposed not to stick in the mind of urban
Late-century man. Keep those for the mutter
Of folk-memory, children's books, history.

In time one can ignore anything, illusion,
Fact. The itch of sound, restless,
Relentless, was lulled into the inoffensive
Breathings of the dark, water, the stress
Of leaves, the quick clinks that birds give.
Sleep brought its welcome fake solution.

The Shock of Distance

The street rushes inward
Wall to wall, narrows
By the minute as the day's
Traffic clots, swills and clots
Again in a jostle of halts.
Air thickens almost to a solid.

Eyes swivel only to cope
With immediates, with where
To put a footstep, how to clear
A coming shoulder, when to hazard
A dodging run in a blizzard
Of brake creaks and wheelslip.

If suddenly a head tilts
Back, pulled by the clinks
Of scaffolders niggling a bank's
Huge facade, the shock
Of distance comes in a quick
Look in a gap into the vaults

Of low sky and the agile
Line of hills, chalked with sleet,
Lifting above the end of the blocked street:
Opening now on a different
Destination, trackless and hesitant,
The wind floundering across every mile.

That is not where people are.
It does not invite
Ambition's bitter spurt or the sweat
Of a long holding on; only troubles
With a wilderness of possibles
The cramped, determined roadway roaring here.

Three Fires

1. *Moor Fire*

The sky signalled it. Sunset streaks flared
Out an hour behind time and in the
Wrong direction, followed by a faint
Premonitory sniff of thickened
Air weaving through the dark. Then the long
Hill quivered into vivid orange.

No harsh gasp of flame or rattle of
Trapped, tindery bracken could reach us
Over a two-mile gap. Writhing
Heather-stalks cracked and roared in the mind's
Ear. Now and then, plainly, a gorse-bush
Grenaded into sparks.
                              Drifts of smoke
Wavered over the aerials of
The indifferent valley, whose glassed-in
People swam in a dim protective
Light, and sipped reality filtered
Through a screen.
                              Above on the raging
Hill the edge of fire jabbed onwards towards
The farms. Small groups of choking figures
Beat at it doggedly with wet sacks.

2. *Barn Fire*

We were wakened by the urgency
Of cries, one voice to another over
Fields in the night, a disturbance
Needling light sleepers.

The window was strangely lit with
Unsteady reddened air which worried
Us alert. Behind sharp trees
A waterfall of flame poured up and up

Angering the sky. Sprays of fire
Trailed down the wind and faded,
Or dropped out of sight. Somewhere
Cattle maintained a bemused complaint.

Firemen's yellow helmets ghosted along
Hedges, looking for watercourses.
As if disorientated, blind, tractors
Snorted behind weaving headlights.

Next day the duty crew stood
In the yard with the farmer, under
A gaunt stone barn, roofless and
Smoking. They did not speak to

Outsiders, but sweated together
Quietly. Spread round them in the open
A world of black hay stank in ruin,
Astonishing Sunday walkers.

3. *City Fire*

Ahead of us the traffic slows,
And halts, and no one knows
At first what's going on. A clearance ·
Area, most of it unlived-in,
Houses ripe for coming down.
The red gleam of a fire-appliance.

Hoses slack and flat on the street
Buck and swell as a waterjet
Hammers into an empty house
Through a hole in the roof.
Coiled smoke rolls out of
Downstairs windows, and loose

Net curtains, still drooping
There, yellowed, take wing
In a sudden flared brilliance
And disappear. Hardly visible
In the noon dazzle small
Flickers on the roof get up a dance.

Next door the house is occupied.
A dismal group of white-eyed
Indians stares up at the slates.
You can't be sure, against the mild
Unclouded blue, how wild
The dance is, or how firm the jets.

Tom Robinson

I remember a one-armed miller, a man
Floured even to his moustache,
So that whenever he moved or spoke
He was haloed in a dry mist.
The hook he had for a left arm
Was versatile for a hook. In all
His work he was deft, agile among
His machinery, in a mill so old
The cogwheels were made of wood.

This miller had been skilled beyond
The management of water and wheel,
Beyond the staple of his grinding.
Neighbours spoke of his occasional
Cradling in his one arm of a gross
Old muzzle-loader. He would
Prime it with a small steel ball
His son used as a marble, then
Stroll to his dam and watch the water
Patiently as a heron.

After as long as an hour he used to raise
The single barrel slowly on his hook,
Aiming down at the blank skin of the water.
There would be more waiting in a dead
Still world. The muzzle stared with its one eye.
Then a rip of flame joined gun
To leaping water, a slamming roar
Jumped back off the trees and mill-wall,
And up from the rocking deep, white-bellied
And still as a log, rolled a huge dead pike.
The boy got his marble back. Every time.

Word of this spun round the county
And wove a myth the neighbourhood
Still wound about him in his eighties,
When the long gun hung undusted on the wall.
The pale old eye, earlier gifted
With that fabled infallible accuracy
Tensioning a harmony of variables,
Looked over the unmoving legendary water
As if no history lay submerged at all.

As if he were a near-retiring
One-armed miller with a white moustache,
Efficient still but getting past it
Like the wood-wheeled mill, whose only
Role had been to grind and grind and do
Expected ordinary things. Instead of moving
Within the outline of another man
Shimmering round him in the flour dust,
Who in his life made one thing perfect
And with that shattering accomplishment
Of floating fish and gasping friends, strode
Almost anonymously into fame.

Scotchman's Stump
(A memorial close to the television mast on Winter Hill)

Fifteen hundred feet above the sea
Glinting in cloud-gaps thirty miles away
Beyond the Mersey Bar,
The pillar stands where he died.
A short stump of iron, holding
To his memory an inscribed plate:

William Henderson, traveller,
A native of Annan, Dumfriesshire,
Barbarously murdered
On Rivington Moor
At noonday in November
In eighteen hundred and thirty-eight.

On this ground where the clubs
Thudded down, and his head
Broke under crushed defending fingers,
He dropped to the tussocked grass.
Near him, pools of dark peat-water
Grew slow spirals of red.

This is where his life's track and the ambush
Locked, after whatever wheeling incomputable
Configurations clicked into place
And doomed him, wandering from Annan
Over this clouded hump. It is a suitable
Haunt for the violent. For storms, for men.

Now from the television mast,
From a thousand feet, the staywires
Drop, thick as thighs, and plunge
Into the ground, anchored,
Slabbed with concrete, deep
Under the embedded heather.

The mast drags eyes up its white leap
To the sky, away from his eight-foot
Iron pillar, black, dark as the landscape,
Jutting like a crude thorn. The rage
Of his killing is rooted yet,
In the earth's bulk and indifference.

He died, the inscription states,
In the twentieth year of his age.

La Gran'mère du Chimquière
(A statue-menhir in a Guernsey churchyard)

You are a gatepost, a sentry
guarding the short path to the porch
the packed graveyard and the yews.
Granite, smoothed by ages of weather,
rippling under the hand's wandering touch.

Cracked across by some tremendous
blow, and then mortared whole,
your body carries for ever the wound
taken in the angry days, a deacon's
hammer breaking you, the idol

dangerous yet after centuries,
a lure for children's posies, brushed
for luck by the sick and the disappointed.
Your face can still be conjured to a smile
above the woman shape just

varying the long thick slab of stone.
You stood somewhere on this site
through twenty-five centuries,
the church choosing the same holy ground,
the cemetery spreading at your feet.

Then the strict hammer swung and stopped
your leaking from a kept-locked past.
Mother-figure, concentratedly
complex, you dropped from goddess to
gatepost, stuck with hinges, stained with rust.

A Student Drama Group Performs in an Old People's Home

Early evening sun leaned through the window
And warmed the carpet under their bare feet.
Powder hazed the room, and make-up sticks
Jumped heavily from clutch to clutch. Clothing
Smothered chairs, and strained plastic bags
Burst in impatience spilling properties out.

Young men aged their temples, and girls
Trenched their incipient wrinkles with thick paint.
Outside the room the corridor unrolled
Itself to life, as walking-frames and sticks
Hauled slow feet to this evening's destination.
Lost, querying voices wavered and fell,

Fell into silence in the dressing-room
Where ironies oozed tangible as sweat:
The low light from the window gilded arms
Roundly lifting from flurries of lawn, to crush
Bright hair under grey acrylic wigs.
They moved in mirrors with a shocked grace.

The cast followed the same corridor down
To the same end, to the room where the audience
Waited. Full-fleshed and springing under
Their flabby mimicry, they strode in
And hurried straight to the front to be looked at,
Vital, and shadowed now under a new guilt.

And afterwards the matron said that they
All had enjoyed it, residents and staff.
'And now I have to help to bed the ones
Who can't walk back to their little flats.
Thank you again, we like these changes here.
Next week, you know, we have the acrobats.'

The Scholar Speaks, in Her Retirement

I once had tea with Otto Jespersen.
We had been in correspondence. Things
In the manuscript of *Beowulf*
(Cotton Vitellius) I saw as pointers
To readings in the Middle English *Pearl*.
I was a graduate student then, a girl.

I called, naturally it was at his
Suggestion, one late summer afternoon
At his country home in Western Denmark,
Walking from the station. He was most
Welcoming. He cut a dark brown cake.
Later he took me rowing on the lake.

His arms were sinewy, curiously brown,
I thought, for a scholar's, I don't know why; eyes
Of distinct blue. We travelled smoothly
In hot light. I felt I should have had
A parasol. The sun, starting to die,
Recklessly oranged almost half the sky.

He paid delicate compliments to my
Scholarship. The oars were entering in
And lifting, entering in again,
Dripping crystals of light. The water
Rolled back like silk sheets. Still,
It was all so still, round our boat's small turmoil.

I left him late, almost at nightfall. My head
Was turning with the stimulus of talk.
Any philologist would have envied me;
To be received by Jespersen, and shown
Such courtesy. He walked me to the train,
And shook hands. We did not meet again.

Across the half a century of my own
Modest achievement, I have held those hours
And those colours, the blues, the browns, the clean
Unfolding waters. All my researches were
A rediscovering at whatever cost
Of what I found there; or of what I lost.

The Royal Charter

*(Wrecked off the coast of Anglesey in October 1859
on returning from the Australian goldfields)*

Carried in moneybelts, snug,
rubbing against the skin for weeks,
months, a conspiratorial

discomfort hugged jealously tight,
becoming a natural outgrowth
modifying the waist like age:

it was gold dust, packed hard, heavy,
swept from Kalgoorlie in a shrewd,
crazed, committed rush, history

made and a country mapped in passing.
To win is sometimes, most times,
unbelievable. The belt's grip told

and told of triumph, held it
closer than clothing, at last, at last,
itchy, incontrovertible, secure.

Land, for stepping onto, slid by
to starboard, there for stepping onto.
The last night came, the last, tense sleep.

Wheeling out of the Atlantic, or out
of nowhere but the clenched knowing
that it had to, had to come,

the vicious wind, the worst for years,
for a century, waves, huge as churches,
steepled them to the clouds, then flung,

slammed them into the foamed rocks,
buckling, bursting the plates, throwing
all of them ashore, some gasping alive,

most dead, sprawled in their wild finish.
Twenty-five yards from the shore they drowned,
fingers stretched out for the pounded

pebbles. They were strewn for miles, miles,
patterning the beaches, stiffening,
locked in certainties, promises, moneybelts.

A Separate Peace

They have found a place, these two,
Utterly unassailable.
A third of the way down the cliff
Above the bump and shuffle of the tide
They lodge with a cushion of heather
On a table-sized rock. Behind them
The private solidity of granite:
Before them the vast hemispherical
Vacancy.
A few gauze clouds, at a height
That almost forbids relationship
With the unflecked slab of sea, are
Thinning themselves into nothing.

Only from a promontory of unconsidered
Stony irregularities and weed masses
Are they observable, aloft
In their achieved autonomy.
Here they commit themselves
To themselves, curtained by cliff
From everything but the nearly
Empty light. And when they enfold
Each other in their conspicuously
Separate peace, what shines out
Is the thin track they have arrived by
And must return along, precarious,
Worn by others, a necessary scar.

Visitor

Your Massachusetts vowels glided
over the table like alien birds.
Your fork right-handed prodded
inexpertly to my eye among
the slices of beef and the obligatory
Yorkshire pudding. England for visitors.

But the talk was of somewhere else,
of home naturally, that for you was
Alaska now, where your husband flew
helicopters for the oilfields rattling
day by day away over a big landscape.
Yours a grey life, with a **thread** of strain.

The wet cold was the worst, you said. Like this
in England, take off some degrees. You'd sooner
fry in Phoenix Arizona for a lifetime;
at least you can get out of Phoenix,
you're locked in Juneau. Small-town living
in that big landscape. You wanted out.

That's how it is for most of us, perhaps.
Whether ice or scrub or drab lawn fills
the window it abuses us and we
want out. Somewhere an opposite must
loose us into joy, the sweat or shivers
eased, the grey breaking into brilliance.

Evening and your leaving in thick drizzle
packed you into the car. Come see us
you said anytime you're over. Any
time I'm in Alaska, then, I have
a home to visit. Bear-steaks and sockeye.
Huge freedoms. We waved you away, steering

into the wet cold, over the small landscape.

Position

I slept with my head on a bag of bullets
At one stage. It was a habit I had
For a stretch of my life, arising from what
You might perhaps call the weather
In the place where I was at the time.

A linen draw-string bag with fifty rounds
Grinding gently together behind my ears
Was less of an irksome pillow than might be
Thought. I could for a long time balance
Easily on the edge of sleep, and neither fall

Relaxing back into blackness nor awkwardly
Shift, wakeful and comfortless, awaiting alarms.
Resting on bullets was reasonable given
The shadows of the hard stars of that country
And the noises asking attention in the night hours.

Now that I no longer (more than most)
Live among small-arms, I try to recall
Whenever I can the wary ease of that
Sharp creaking pillow. Shadows gloom as furtive,
And the night sounds grow the more insistent here.

Scars

A miner climbed from his car,
closed the door with a soft
locking thump, and skinned
his gloves off. Dark blue scars
crossed the backs of his hands;
another extended an eyebrow
onto a cheek.
           His life
was signed by his work, as others
too are scored by what
if anything they have moved through,
inwardly holding scars
as permanent, endured
as they have to be, if not
worn with such indelible aplomb.

Gravestone

Sergeant Armfield was buried here
In the forties, brought from Scotland
Sealed and beflagged in a coffin.
He had the full treatment, slow-march,
Firing-party, press photographs.

And there was private grief. A girl
From Arran, parents with their lives
Collapsed now, the shuffling neighbours.
His body had been in the sea
For weeks, missing, washed from his launch.

An Air-Sea Rescue coxwain, he
Patrolled the Great Lakes, and later
The Channel, then the Western Isles.
He was known, they said, for his cold
Skill in prising away pilots

Jellied to their controls, or in
Hoisting others out of the sea
Fried black and floating, while his crew
Were left to be guiltily sick,
Clutching the guard-rails, eyes elsewhere.

Nineteen years old, he had left here
A boy and returned a drowned man.
Died on Active Service. The stone
Holds the last tenth of his life, spent
Lifting the living and the dead.

Now

'No man steps into the same river twice.'
—Heraclitus

Fording a river compels a thought.
Of what has been said before concerning
Rivers and stepping into them, neat
Gem-like observations that we never
Experience the shock of the same thing
Twice. Always it is different water.

In a way the classic aphorism states
The irrelevant. The current rushes its hard
Clarity over the shallows, and the boots'
Heavy confidence grinds against the stones'
Uncertain bed; the opposite side
Means simply what this crossing means.

But as the deepening river climbs
To the knees and curls back over its weight,
A glance downstream from the middle seems
Like the pull of history. The instant terrifies
By never being here. Upstream the bright
Enormous waters headlong fill the eyes.

The Fountain

In the municipal gardens, near
The ornamented gates, a fountain
Hangs like a silver willow
Trailing its arms across the backs of goldfish:
A tree so engineered that all
Its living, all its dying, moves
Arching and falling in a fixity.
The top twigs flicking in the sun
Stand fast, and slip down boughs
To splash their ends and slip
Deep to the pageant of revolving fish.

On the parapet a man of ninety
Sits, eating his sandwiches,
Facing the sunlight on the slate roofs
Lumped with pigeons, and the city
That sprawls on its elbows into where was green,
Blowing its tainted breath before it.
Back to the springing waters
He feeds the sparrows scrapping for his crumbs.

A row of greasy ribbons stands in his coat.
Where is the striding soldier was his youth
That marched through Frontier suns and sweat
His fear to bugles?
Eager mindsight has him
Curve backward from this culmination
And gleam continuous to the topmost reach,
Real as the shape of this great hanging water.

A trim thought to hold a lifespan
Present like a fountain's column,
All his days' drops tracked
And dazzling in their still descent,
The whole arc visible behind him.
The athlete in the khaki topee leaps
From rock to rock and the crack
Of rifles splits the heat of this
Same sun that warms his knuckles now.

Where this man's reality is
Is a query needing such a trick
Of light, making seventy years
A filled space, a graspable
Totality; needing a film dissolve
From soldier to this, from sandwiches
To rifle bolt, superimposed
Translucent images. But he rolls
His wrapping paper, slings it in a bin,
And leaves the fountain snickering behind him.
His past too swims in the gills
Of gaudy fishes, under the splashes
Of insistent now. And oddly time,
Time that should bring the belly scream,
Dances in splatters and a tattered coat.

Linkages

She poured out greenish water
from the tub which had held all day
her celebratory bouquet.
It went with her wild laughter

galloping into the tight drain
but backed up over the top
of the bowl to slither and drop
on her thighs in a rush of rain.

The flowers, propped in the hot
dry air, looked unconcerned.
They kept their stems together, leaned
on the wall and leaked from their feet.

They stood firmly in the crowded
indifferent contingent world,
though centred on a shelf to enfold
what meaning the moment had.

Triumph for her will always now
wallow in greenish water
leaping from all the world she saw to
shock her warm skin into an icy glow.

Persistence

The thick gurgling bleat
of a camel loaded
and goaded to its feet
beside a railway track
in the enormous black
and white starlit
desert clarity

this will come back
and again come back
with the smell of oiled
steel mixed with oranges
and the need for silence –
like the membrane of a balloon
thinned to bursting point –

then the cracked-out orders
and what could have ended
differently ended as it did
and the sun boiled up loose
over the saw-edged mountains
and the balloon breathed out
slowly and for a long time.

Superimposing

Cold waters the eyes
    and slits them shut.
Out of the market
    big squares of paper
empty boxes fruit wrappings
    sail on the wind
and startle traffic
    some of them swirling
high over everything
    lodging on rooftops
with the hunch of vultures.

    Dogs get at dustbins
overturned near the stalls
    like hyenas
in African suburbs. They lick
    avidly, slyly.
The pineapple smell
    thickens and grit
under the collar sticks
    like prickly heat.

Bring a gun,
    scare the hyenas
from the yards, wait
    for the imagined first
big drops of rain
    the hot wind is bringing.

Committee Men

It would be better without words,
They shift so eloquently.
Switch off the sound, turn it
From drama to mime. Look at

The dominant one, hunching
Well over the table, elbows
Planting his claim, cancelling
The reasoning persistence of his smile.

Leaned back, chair at the limit
Of tilt, his adversary points his beard
Insultingly at the other's
Eyeballs, his own half-veiled.

Some of them give reminders
Of themselves by knocking pipes out
Or pushing back chairs to cross legs.
Tensely they assert their ease.

Thinking in numbered paragraphs
Is a telling skill. It signals
Control, it has the precision
Of death-sentences: such finality.

One or two vague-minded lightweights
Watch through the window the dance
Of wagtails on the lawn, or a sky
Scattered with loose clouds

Where the wind is carelessly
Erasing the shining contrails
Of people getting somewhere,
Miles above their heads.

Afternoon with a Minor Official

From his assertive Afghan coat
His quick timidity
Hesitated into speech.
His voice grew louder, calmer; soon,

Developing a smooth delivery,
He malapropped his way
Across the afternoon.
When the sad light outside the window

Sagged and dwindled, he tapped a switch.
The glass went black,
The outer world was gone,
And looking there we saw only ourselves

And the posturing complacent
Fringes of his sleeves
Reflecting and reflecting,
Doubling and doubling his performance.

The Avenue

In the hardware shop on the Avenue,
Which being on the Avenue
Is known as the Home Improvement Centre,
They offer a Bargain for Spring.
It is stuck round with daffodils
To show that it is for Spring:
A cordless carpet cleaner
With suction-action brush; a small battery
Powers it. With this, your home
Knows Spring.

Maybe. On the Avenue, they hardly
Know Spring. The odd chaffinch
With its not very frequent, not very
Tuneful song, reminds some,
I suppose. But the hedged-in daffodils
Have a perfunctory look, and could be
Plastic. Like those celebrating the Bargain.
On the Avenue, only acquisitions
Record the seasons. There, they mark
The world's turning with a new buy.

Character Sketch

Pregnant and uncertain of herself.
Exults that as her body
Rounds in its strict obedience, her
Mind is free. Whatever future
Announces itself hourly, crouched
Naked and unknown, bulking
Earnestly within her stretching skin,
Now she knows herself changeless.
Trembles invisibly in case this is not so.

Reflection

Narcissus wasn't the only one.
That sharp and static image
He planted himself to look at
Has other postulants.
                    Not all
Use ponds, or glass, or camera lenses,
Or a diary. Some lure another
To give back that desired
Projection, exact and clear.

This is a fidelity they call
Love.
        Whose full-lipped self
Lifts easily to the face
Lowering to meet it, to touch, to kiss,

And drink the mirror in.

The Gold Bracelet

She lifts her wrist and drinks
and again and again
finds her bracelet's shine,

swinging its heavy links
audibly against one another
through the complaisant air.

Owning is bold to show
itself, of course, but held
in those lumps of gold

there is something more than the glow
of wealth, more than the charm
pulling her own gaze to her arm.

Identity is a cruelly
nebulous thing to hold.
She lifts her wrist and is told

again and again that she
lives, visible, extolled,
in the soft clashing of gold.

Casualties

The purr of the train smoothed
those intricate little noises that prickle
out of a journey's quiet. The slack
time of day was dumb and empty.

The woman's voice broke out high,
too distant down the coach for sense,
but arching, arching in questions.
Her man slumped, shoulder to pane.

Her words went whizzing in but drew
no answer. She expected none.
Each query was an accusation,
a missile or a short-arm jab.

I had watched a magpie hammering
a box, driven by the hollow knock
into an ecstasy of conviction
that here was a discovery of gold.
The box was empty.
                    The dull man sat,
watching the stricken elms of England
pass and pass like walking wounded.

Event

To crunch a first bite
into the almost
white, close-packed inside
of a fresh-pulled big
lettuce, feeling it
crackle on the teeth,
knowing the surely
tangible goodness
of pure composted
growing, and finding
the tongue suddenly
slide over the sleek
and gelatinous
globule of a slug

causes an abrupt
staggering of thought,
a rushing surge of doubt
in gardens, nature,
good, the divine plan.
Spat out and surpised
it lies on a stone,
satisfied. Newton's
apple accomplished
something similar.

No inductive laws
follow the slug, though.
Failing a taste for
rearranging all
reality, what
can be done but bite
a fresh bite, having
to endure it all
as it is, fearing,
daring that the next
slug could be impaled
on an eye-tooth. Yes,
to go on biting
seems the only thing.
Into the obscure
hard and folded heart.

Stimulus

You make a Calcutta of my head;
a million alleys narrow as
capillaries, crammed with the din of
living, blocked by the dead.

Sweating, I twist and struggle to turn
architect, one able to open
the crushed city to a scouring wind,
striding in with a plan.

I wish I carried inside my skull
a Canberra, tribute to logic,
looping, tree-thick, rich in distances,
and geometrical.

Still, if you were different from what
you are, there'd be no steaming city
crouching round its despair. I'd have no
drive to bulldoze the lot,

no muscled patience, no stretching gaze
towards Canberra from my Calcutta.
Instead, the small-town featureless streets
I'd built and now despise.

Feud

A fox with a collar, fat, quiet,
  bell-under-chin, sat by the roses
on a small lawn and hung
  a tongue over its teeth.
Target enough, this one. Inside
  sloped the boy in leather,
leaving his bike, going back
  for his other technology.
Out with his gun, twelve-bore,
  loaded, aimed from a few
feet, exploded. The fox was lifted
  among the roses, kicking,
tongue still hanging, spread
  with flower-heads and an enormous wound.

Beside the bar, blood dried and stiff,
  swung from its nape, gaping
above its chest, it was held for
  gawping at. Mount the head
at least, they said. The collar,
  the bell, the owner's name-tag,
lay quietly elsewhere. There are
  dangers in kinship, even
collared; red leather and a bell,
  the brand of property, hold back
no gunman's glee. Denaturing
  does not indemnify. Intruder
among the roses, round and still,
  he ranks with his quick lean brothers from the hill.

Epic Simile

In the way that a change of light,
For instance from a shift
In the configuration of clouds, but more
From the switching-on of a room-lamp
At evening, after the colours lit
By the sunset have calmed down,
Robs startlingly the appearances of things
So that carpets, shoe-leather, pot-plants
Languish as other than they were, as now
They are, dim, unremarkable, routine,
In just that way an altered expectation,
As from a silent phone, or letter forcing
A second stunned incredulous read,
Drains off the temporary sunglow
From those who had moved richly in it,
Therefore supposed elect.
                              As Virgil knew,
The art of seeing often lies
In correspondences, quick to slide one
Out from under gilding patinas
Straight into monochrome chill air,
Quick to unglaze the eyes to look
In plain light at what is plainly there,
To welcome a sudden closing
Of the sky, and slyly watch
A hand reach out to the protective switch.

Overhearing

The loneliest voice I heard as a child
was the moaning of telegraph poles
on a two-mile stretch of road, white
and straight as a taut string,
a road lying over a wild
gorse-cluttered common, between low walls.

The multiple hum, the packed chord
of the poles and the pots seemed, were,
had to be the milling conversations
of the communicators, town to town,
spilling into the wind each stretched word
out of the loops of swinging wire.

The summer wind pushed back and forth up there
between the poles. Its warmth curled
over the electric voices, but would not
smother the cries of the desolate callers
yearning from town to town. The air
trembled with all the agonies of the world.

The wind was in the end the stronger,
turning explanatory, blowing chill.
The squeezed allowances of speech
leaking from within the thin wire links
cooled to simple movements of the air:
themselves more primitive, and lonelier still.

Falling Asleep

Lion country is of the mind, too.
Even when the huge confusing herds,
Zebra, wildebeeste, innumerable
Leaping gazelles, even when they all
Eventually lose themselves over
Yellowy grass, then the darkness comes.
Suddenly, without twilight, the fierce
Unsettling stars are in position.

This is not a land for exploring.
Hooves and horns have wandered across it,
Every hunted beast has sniffed its air.
Remembered now in the insistent
Light of the stars, other toothed creatures,
Alien and demoralising,
Needling the ground with their stealthy claws,
Draw their feet up under them to spring.

Determined

Travelling in necessary or chosen places,
Whether for instance in a baked and shambling
Train in the East, or perhaps
Balancing foot after foot on a goat-path
Making its way up out of the atmosphere
Above the last of the trees, one often
Feels that the world might generously
Have offered easier routes than these.

Circling the mind is the irritant
Saving notion that chance has had
Something to do with it, however
Far back, decisions casual as coffee,
Taken on utterly different things,
Leading at last to here. That's the knack
Of contingency, laying the future down
Tight as this foetid or lung-emptying track.

Pragmatism

Acres of foot-high pines are bristling
Round the farms that for years had
Only the tufted moorland
Rolling about them in the wind.
They make a low green mist, these trees,
Denser every season; they are whistling
Interminably their dull adagios.

Next year and the next again those
Mercantile intruders will extend
Their claim on air, on the eye's competence,
On all the kingdom of the ear, and bend
Perception into modes the senses
Grow to season after season. Habit
Welds on, undramatic as daylight.

The squat stone houses, built tight
And thick against the leaning wind,
Will loll in a mild retreat beneath
The forest wall, ranks of thickened
Trunks blocking the distance. The breath
Of pines, resinous, close, will relax
The bruised purpose, the bemused assent.

Divisions

The parks at one time
all had railings round them,
spiked and close-fitting.

A clock near the gate was set
to show closing-time. Only
darkness was allowed in then.

The scrapyards swallowed
the railings, the authorities
their misgivings. Lots of air

escaped and came rolling
over the grass and out
into the roads. People walked in,

anywhere, all along the boundary.
Where were the edges of things? Life
wandered, lost, into little freedoms.

Cities and Dogs

You know a city by its walking dogs.
They form a kind of moving furniture
To complement the static pillar-box,
Tram-stop and litter-bin, grace-notes
Above the motifs of the architecture.

In Amsterdam the schnauzers, matt
Black and bristly, lugging on chains young men,
Nudge through the shoppers on the Kalverstraat.
Their muscled-tee-shirt owners, louche and loping,
Are epochless and cosmopolitan.

St Andrews, northwards, seemly and sedate,
Has gundogs padding up the Scores in twos,
With a secure, well-regulated gait,
Noses to ground and half a pace behind
Some thick twill trouser cuffs and solid shoes.

In Amsterdam not much is not absorbed.
A freak of gables fringing a canal
Can watch farouche intruders undisturbed.
St Andrews likes its stubble-coloured friends
Nosing along below the dead cathedral.

Sotto Voce

Whispering is an art that some few
Never master. Their physical
Equipment fails, they are like
Those who cannot whistle, yodel,
Or ever learn to ride a bike.

Speaking out, though, is a virtue
Often spoken out about.
It is a buoyant skill
That carries the appropriate
Voices, firm or shrill,

And those who hear, those too
Who overhear, are not in mind
Much. What counts is clearance,
Flinging out the self, leaving behind
A settling turbulence.

Sad, then, that in their view
The subtleties they cannot reach
Lie as malevolence beyond
Permitted boundaries of speech.
For them the truth is what is megaphoned.

Young Man at a Party

Perhaps the aloof one there,
Holding himself up tall,
Is secretly, greedily bolder,
Looking at all the hair,
Imagining how it might fall,
Perhaps, on his moonlit shoulder.

Maybe, though, when he maps
Out his terra incognita,
Nothing is marked but Dragons; he eyes
Their reeking nose-holes with surprise,
Knowing he's out too far,
So staying aloof, perhaps.

Women in Gardens

The quick flawing of an even sky
by a flight of hell-bent pigeons
brings into the mind a helicopter view
of all the houses, and the gardens
dotted with women sporadically
wrestling the washing, and prams
wailing on the shabby grass.

Lives are established like
the small trees on the north
sides of the houses, leaning
desperate for light, straining out
after a rumour of sun, yearly
stretching to top the roofs and break
at last into a dazzle of air.

And year by year the indelible
pressure of children, from pram
to swing to bicycle to car
to disappearance, swift
as the vanished pigeons,
leans on the women under
the droop of trees, the smoothly clouded sky.

Sons, Departing

They walked away between tall hedges,
their heads just clear and blond
with sunlight, the hedges' dark sides
sickly with drifts of flowers.

They were facing the sea and miles
of empty air; the sky had high
torn clouds, the sea its irregular
runs and spatters of white.

They did not look back; the steadiness
of their retreating footfalls lapsed
in a long diminuendo; their line
was straight as the clipped privets.

They looked at four sliding gulls
a long way up, scattering down frail
complaints; the fickle wind filled in
with sounds of town and distance.

They became sunlit points; in a broad
haphazard world the certain focus.
Against the random patters of the sea
their walk was one-directional, and final.

Implications

There is a kind of silence
that stored apples make
when they decorate the floor
of a dim attic,
holding subdued colours
that you know about but see
only in the thick wine of their smell.

These coloured silences wrap
wholeness up, latent,
smelling of memory. The dull
floor would hollowly knock
at the drop of a knuckle,
the rock-tight apple-skins
could be polished to nuggets.

All is there in the lack
of sound, the full recall
of what could be, packed
there solid as apples, the known
knock of wood, the dusted
sheen of slick fruit, the air
misty with imagined juices.

Sad Men
(The woodcuts of Harry Stirrup)

Their necks lack gristle
to position the skull.
Weight leadens their eyelids; hung
jawbones accept the earth's pull.
Their mouths give up and sag open.

Space claims them and frames them
tight. They shrink closely more
closely into themselves, they hug
nothing but their knees. Their
singleness is rapt and complete.

Over their worked skins
the tooling has laid scars
turned gentle as leaves, as light,
fluttering over the lean torsos,
solacing the taut limbs.

Craft has cut its way
through to them, has discovered
their grief. Signs of the struggle
are gouged in the woodgrain. Levered
out of the encounter rises love.

Defining an Absence

This is to walk squinting into a sun
 which edges everything wintrily
with incredible hardness, even
 grass-stalks frosted into still
sabres bristling at the bottoms of walls,
 the walls themselves given
such uncompromising presence
 their weight is known as never before.

And never before have footsteps
 been like the tapping of a door
someone has gone out through and left loose
 in a cool wind, defining an absence
no sun will ever do anything to
 but sharpen like the sabres of the grass,
or plant as firmly in the early light
 as these blank formidable walls.

Modes

Gull in a glint
of sun in the quick
turn of noon
arraigns that tick
of time, that hairline
watershed;
provides a hint
in easy flick
with wing and head
of daylight's down-
ward slide to the wreck
of sunset.

Gull in a storm
hangs to the back
of a bucking wind
above the smack
and smother on land
of driven sea;
and here is room
within the lock
of conflict, grey
space to find
around the clock
no end to day.

Endings

Ash lies cold and unsmoking
Just the colour of the damp daybreak
Undistinguished from the dull grass
Pieces of wood stones debris
Of a dead fire.
              Not a nugget
Of heat no minutest jewel
Delays and offers a glow
Holds a remote heartbeat
Energising a hope a scorch
Clear enough to tingle the skin
Of a plunged fingertip.
                  The moist
Amorphous chill cushion of ash
Fails to respond with more than
Sifting resistance as the daylight
Rises and compels acceptance
Admission of the ruin
The nothing the finality.

The Consolations of Colours

The waste-basket chokes white
swallowing the calendar's
tear-off leaves.

Inevitably death informs
red, tracing maples
through falling woods.

Blue is icily immense,
for astronauts turning
to total black.

House-smoke pillaring the sky
on silent days
inscribes ash-grey epitaphs.

Green, even, is corrosive;
at the beginnings of springs
it washes hedgerows with acid.

The Glass Barrier

The eyes are round but unperturbed,
the jaws gulp without surprise,
the fins work ceaselessly but not
in agitation; beyond the glass
the signs read differently.

That nonchalance, those flicking
turns, all the time bejewelling
the fronded water-plants, they are
not skills but plain belonging,
where to belong is to be beautiful.

Here in the hollow corridor
stabbed by the neon windows
of the tanks, the shadow urges
a baffled leaning towards the glass,
the air-clear final barrier.

One inch through and they would
suffocate, the shubunkins shawled
in their gauzy tails, as we should drown.
We eye and mouth remotely, their lit space
sleek and unreachable as youth will be.

Presences

This eight-lane highway slams along
the scrublands. Gulleys flick
past, each one condemned in
concrete.

A century will accede to this,
tending its white certainty,
learning its restructured
landscape.

Here the Navajo always moved
silently, flexible skins
on their feet, their small horses
unshod.

They buried their embers under
inches of earth. They unpiled
piled stones and healed their
trenches.

Crossing the country they were
as flying geese, offering
as little disturbance.
They were

less evident than wind,
traceless as river salmon
in big water. Even
their smoke

brushed fadingly against
the trees that fuelled it.
Honouring everywhere, they left
no tracks.

Perception

Considering the way that dogs go
Lolloping across the park on Sundays
(And every other day they get the chance)
I wonder how the inhabitants of the grass
React, the mice, the big-eyed rabbits,
Even the seasonally travelling fox.
Most of them are of course nocturnal,
Out of the way.
                    But sometimes at dawn the dogs
Overlap the dark, ravenous for smells
Recent from a world of marvels their slant
Eyes never fix on, nor white teeth grip.

Rituals

They spit words like raw sloes
from puckered mouths: you can see
the women in the windy lane
heads forward hacking their men;
it is Sunday, Sunday.

They come back, the men, from sitting next
to the strict canal, rods fixed
at their feet, a concentration like love
on the orange floats hovering above
the promise in the water.

To the houses they come, late,
in their eyes remnants of that
otherness the women hate,
the hint of a world apart,
a hazed indifference.

Ritual on this day succeeds
ritual; an array of cries abrades
the evening, but unannulled
is the rapt, tight wait for the revealed,
for the lifting, imaginable shine.

Late-Night Bus Station

Overhead lighting clanks in the wind.
Torn bits of shadow run up walls
And over the wet ground
Within an amber glow that cancels
What colours there are.

The gasp and shudder of a bus
Ready to lumber away shakes loose
The glue between lovers. They uncoil
Into chill singleness, congeal
As two travellers.

On the platform a wavering drunk
Hangs to the handrail as if
Riding a freighter flung
About by the wild Atlantic
Under rocking stars.

The deck heaves into a hill then
Dizzyingly drops from his feet
As she pitches, and the rain
Spills from the gutter in a great
Sobering shower.

He drags his sickness away to where
Home must be. Buses' big tyres share
Puddle water with him as they pass.
Heads leaning on the window-glass
Hold separate stares.

Rugby League Country

1.

The hanging gull
high in the winter air
bends a cold eye
downwards
to the grey-green field

where red mites, white mites
mill and commingle,
spray out, wheel and congeal
repeatedly
across the short afternoon.

A raucous sighing
like wave-water on stones
lifts and lifts to gull-height
insistently
uncontrollable as sea-noise.

Car roofs cluster shiny
as wet pebbles
dulling when the light dies
gradually.
The gull steers off on stiff wings.

2.

Bruising is bred
                in the bone.
It becomes habit.
                      Among
the runs, mudslides, heart-
                              jarring
blocking collisions, compli-
                                cations
of armlocks and leghooks,
                            kickings
and shire-horse heavings,
                          the aches
grow and gather and grow
                          until noticed
and they take over, winning,
                              and the body
agrees to them, becomes acquiescent,
                                      is a pain-machine.

3.

The street could still be
a thirties street, except
that the only men are old
who fringe it with buckled knees
in the true style, squatting
all afternoon and staring.

Their eyes are hostile
to strangers. Above ground
for years now they still blink
tentatively at the sunlight.
They wait on cold Saturdays
for their sons' cars and the grandchildren.

4.

Two luminous white faces lift
out of scarves in the right colours
for this town. Their eyes pucker
in the blustery cold. His arm adrift
on the sway of her shoulders
trails every indifferent finger.

Security sits in his smile.
Having no need of other
emblazonment, he lets
the colours and complaisant girl
banner his being here, further
his belonging, having his rights.

5.

Gunmetal water, in a canal
straight as a cannon's barrel,
floats among darker debris
two swans

which after a long increasing
wingbeating slide along the top
of the water, lift themselves
airborne

and the rhythm of their passing
low over the sharp rooftops
turns a few faces upward
curiously.

6.

Jeans follow jeans across the bridge.
In the road the bumpers nose close
to one another. Wind rips
the top off the canal. The talk
is gritty as the air, from lips
tight against blue exhaust smoke.

A dog snarls from behind a hedge.
He like his garden turns a morose
wintry eye to the world. Chips
already tickle the wind in the dark
avenue. Jeans lick their lips.
Strides lengthen to a brisker walk.

7.

The outdoor market is a stumble
of thick clothes in narrow
alleys. The wind is flecked with sleet.
Repeatedly the canvas tops billow
and flap or hold in a tense tremble.

A girl with salmon-coloured hands
juggles with silver bars of fish
flopped onto shards of ice. Her neat
blade trims away their bones. A blush
of crabmeat cowers among parsley fronds.

Buffets of huckstering concuss
everyone's ears; the rival shouts
lift out and weave over the street
into the rugby ground's rites. Clouds
of contending sound drop on all of us.

Watching

Guard dogs bellow at the frost.
They quiver their thin pelts and circle,
Ticking their blunt nails on the stone.
Rooftops prickle in points of fire.

Cats flatten themselves to shadows
And two round owls are hooked
Alert onto empty branches. Cat eyes,
Owl eyes, strange-pupilled, night-knowing,

Mock the dogs in the warehouse yard
Slanting their noses upward
Ballooning howls into the dark.
The stars too fix them implacably.

The whole night is like a brain
Febrile with images.
I am afraid to sleep it through,
Would rather shiver like the dogs,

Stare back at the steady owls,
Nose out the sliding shadows,
Watch with the aware stars,
Watch, watch, and not be caught out.

Droplets

In the waves at the lake's edge you were
Bathing at the exact point of daybreak
Given a glitter by the water and by
The suddenly lifting sun a hue
Perhaps of October bracken.

Of all beginnings this was the most
Ceremonious. The creeping
Waves, accommodating, low,
Distributed themselves around
Your wading disappearing knees.

The water you heaved in your hands
To drop across face and shoulders
Like shards of glass, scattered
And rattled back into the surface
Or slid downwards beading your skin.

The melting of those handfuls, those bits
Of spikily reflected sunrise,
Into the homogeneous enclosing
Lake, is what will register as loss,
Later, amid smooth civilities.

Appearance

A hut grew singly out of the grass
Among trees that were almost like it,
Sharing leaves; but those
On the roof of the hut lacked gloss
And were hanging limp. Outside
By the door a boy wearing only a vest
Had rooted his feet
In the soft inch of dust.

He was quiet as the stem
Of a bush. His arms and spread
Fingers held surprise in front of him
Like an unwieldly bundle. And from
His face came a stare, white, wide,
Pulling his head round after us.
But the turn of the road
Sneaked us away from his eyes.

Beyond us, beyond both him and us,
The lilac mountains sixty miles away
Pretended to be touchable; the space
Hung empty, hauling close
The detailed rockface. Never
Despite itself will clarity like that
Alter a distance; nor ever
Lose the pull of its deceit.

Disengaging

Circles of champagne froth show where
dolphins have nosed under the calm
green surface, wheeled their backs
over one last time and gone
deep. This disappearing white
fizz is the last sign of them.

From now on it seems as though
the dull engine boom is all
we can count on for company,
that and occasional cruising
birds. The sea is emptier
for their having been here.

The long horizon rounds and rounds
on everything. It holds in its ring
bewilderment, emptiness over the sway
of a world coiling with aliens,
cold, unblinking. The dolphins had broken
into and out of it, harmonious.

All their lunging agility
their lifting and sliding has now
dropped into the filtered
multifarious light of fathoms
down, coolly releasing from them
the thunder of these abandoned screws.

Curio

Heavy as goodbye
the onyx elephant
levers its carved lines
confidently under the air.

White, the sacred colour,
holds blemishes of rock-grain,
glints, too, of cut light
the craftsman has left to it.

The table top presses
desperately upwards
against it. Its feet
express it. It yearns, yearns

forward into emptiness,
trunk and tusks prodded
out, body packed behind,
but sure of itself, of its feet.

We can trust it in its pure
not quite pure white, its planted
feet firm to lean forward off,
the sad weight it does not disguise.

The Dancers

Twinned in a cell, foetal,
sleeping, they quiver, stir,
stretch into music, uncoil
into singleness; hot-coloured
lights wash them, finger
them apart; each, awakened,

mirrors the other, limb
moving for limb, loose, fluid,
balancing the solemn
chords their bloodstreams beat
against, till catapulted
to the stage's limits they fret

within separate energies,
spotlit, costumes splintering
gold to arc across
the intervening vaults
of shadow, each at a peak entering
a planned tumult of somersaults.

Inside the amniotic
flow of the lightbeams
the moving and the music,
antinomies collide and quibble
and melt into one another as dreams
do, acute and untranslatable.

Everything, locked poise
of feet, handspring, lift
of breast or arch of wrist, grows
crystals of ambiguities, as on
a precise needle-point. They drift,
unstable images, into fusion.

Dancers for the body are
its imagining, a finding out
of what is to be said. Here,
heaving and glazed in sweat, they bring
to the watching darkness a disquiet,
a neural, undeniable knowing.

Watercourse

1.

Two inches deep and clear
  as nothing;
under it the small stones
  shine and are
magnified, mottled brown
  pointed with fire
where the sun strikes;
  follows declivities,
a flotation for grass-seeds
  insects specks of bark,
twisting into interstices
  of gravel, a tryout
for small sounds like
  the interlocking of vocables,
glistening flat and open
  holding some
of the sky's wide shine.

2.

The bubbled silence
  murmuring to itself enfolds
soft flutterings of air, sharp
  birdcries splintering off
the hill's solidity, a tractor's snore,
  the occasional seemingly
indigenous animal musings
  moaning across the pastures.

3.

The shine of a car strikes
    immovably. Already
a radio sheds into the air
    its flakes of music, its
chips of metalled voice.

4.

The river rattles past
    noisiest too in its
shallowest passages, almost
    able to stun
any alien sound.
    Later it scrabbles
at the motorway's even
    drum, climbing just
high enough to scarify
    that loud unmodified moan.

5.

When thickly it curdles
    through small towns
with froth blowing off it,
    opaque as toffee
and slow as November,
    the river loses.
Canalised and culverted
    directed underground
drained dammed utilised
    it enters silence.

6.

Water moves as language
   moves, building, eroding,
interfered with, trafficking
   helplessly with anything,
taking the colour of effluent,
   stifling the life of all
its organisms, flowing
   sterile, dropping inevitably
onward, necessary, dead.

7.

On the delta the marsh grass
   grows with its feet in a film
of light oil. This is the river's gift,
   its reluctant utterance;
colliding with the primal energies
   it limply spreads itself
to muffle the white ferocity of the tide-rip,
   to placate the salt.

Environment

Most cities accede to them now,
Big circles of thick low flowers
On roundabouts, hanging baskets
Along the lintels of banks, arches
Of branches to modify whatever
The weather is, the occasional
Green flash of a planted bomb.
                    Boarded windows,
Roped-off cracked pavements, commemorate
These instant stamens of flame in the long
Echoing of their blast. Step busily
Round the obstruction, enter the cooling
Tunnel of the trees, rake your eyes
Over the beds and beds of steadily
Erupting flowers.

The Hate-Plant

Returning from his work in the shortening
Evenings of the year he went almost
At once into the garden, closed
Behind the house among heavy trees.

The blade of his spade was a gleam
Going slit and slit into the ground
With the rhythm of a pulse.
It went on for hours.

He was protecting a germination
From a single seed, embedded here
Out of the daylight, a sly growth
Stealthy as fungus, nocturnal.

He sliced away at all intrusive
Tendrils of vegetation, raking the topsoil
Clear of cakings of mud, moss, any hint
Of alien greenery in the land of his plant.

As the days darkened the season
Of growing slowly urged
A thick-stemmed, spread-rooted cultivar
Upward into its own huge branches.

There was no one to watch the labouring
Or note the arrival of the grown plant.
By daylight the leaves receded
Gently into an ordered landscape.

Yellow, feathery, hardly there in the weak
Sun, they stood fleshed and grossly spined
Under throbbing starlight, the expanded
Sap-filled force of the hate-plant.

He fed it under the cold dark
With the rancorous scourings of daylight,
Eyes looking through him, doors shut fast,
The villainous smiles of small men.

He gathered carefully out of his heart
The composted heat of circumstance
And crazed the night garden
With its engendering glow.

He promised that some mild day of sunshine
The plant would miraculously solidify,
The rooted ground be shaken, the air split,
The whole neighbourhood affrighted, stunned.

Hereward

A small blue dragonfly
with bands of black
hangs to the shield of a leaf.
I swear he has his eye on me
though I haven't moved
for hours I haven't moved.

I saw him covering the sector
hovering diving hovering again
he began to quarter the reedbed
wings puttering and puttering
coming in low, low
over the flat water.

He must have been looking for me.
His wings whirred like gauze
swinging this way and that
over the reeds and homing in
for surely no other reason
on that broad leaf.

He sits now steady as a bright
brooch on the leaf, but he was lunging
about in air, directing and redirecting
that big glass head to find
me, not easy to find
in the reeds, careful, camouflaged.

The blur of his wings grew louder,
homing in; it was like God watching.
I tried to be ground, green, anything,
leaf, water, transparent, anything.
My breath halted, hands
became claws.

If he could find me, others too.
Reedbeds deep as Burma even
would not be huge enough and would
not hide me long. Seven days,
perhaps not seven, and other
spies would clatter overhead.

I can wait him out.
In four hours the brute sun
will have crept off me. The short
night will be enough. I can wade
splashlessly among the waterweeds
and head for dust, cities, crowds.

Brickwork holds no breeding-places
for dragonflies. The gritty wind
impedes their airmanship. I shall
look safely at faces, windows,
doorways, moving traffic, ready for
a big eye looming over me like this one.

Possibilities

Knifewounds slither out of the dark.
Cramped streets drop into lamplight
black pools of threat. Knots
of marauders debouch from alleys;
not even their eyes glitter.
Their muffled scramble leaves
sprawled figures robbed and trickling.

In the megawatt-lit
kept-open thoroughfares
closed cars shimmy their rear-lights
and vanish. Beacons bat
their eyes.
        Clocks above it all
draw their indifferent slow circles
but look pale.

Interruptions

Across the river the pleasure launches
Jolt on their ropes in the chop on the water
Ungentling the afternoon.
Judiciously the dawn had printed them
On the flattest of mirrors, doubling
Their painted confidence in a perfect
Calm.
     Hours dulled the glass, the full tide
Fell away to joust with an inshore wind,
And they are left to swing and jostle
For balance. They manage. They ride out
Interruptions, skilfully. They
Justify their crafted shapeliness.

Your Hands

Feminine, so foreign to me
in that respect, no other,
they shape themselves about
their steady capabilities.

The world they work in nearly,
not quite, coinhabits
my own blunt-fingered spaces.
Off-centredness leaves each

a privacy still waiting to be won
beyond the flattened ground we have
made certain of. Your hands, wielding
a semiology of self-concern,

offer it for decoding. They reach
daily towards me a new speech.

John Cassidy lives in Lancashire, where he is a lecturer in literature and drama at a tertiary college. His poems have appeared in many magazines and anthologies, and have been broadcast on radio and television. A selection of his work was included in *Poetry Introduction 3* (Faber, 1975).

Cassidy's booklet *The Dancing Man* was the first Poet's Yearbook Award publication in 1977. His first full-length collection, *An Attitude of Mind*, was published by Hutchinson in 1978. Two pamphlets, *Changes of Light* and *The Fountain*, appeared from Bloodaxe in 1979. *Night Cries* is Cassidy's second book-length collection.

Kim Lewis is a printmaker who lives and works on a farm near Bellingham in Northumberland. Formerly the lithographer at the Charlotte Press Printmaking Workshop in Newcastle, she now has her own workshop for stone lithography and block printing. The front cover shows 'Duration', a stone lithograph from an edition of 30. Enquiries: The Riding, Bellingham, Hexham, Northumberland NE48 2DU.